The South High Horseman:

Stories and Poems by a Teen Cowboy

Peter Smith

Monday Creek Publishing

Ohio USA

On the Front Cover: Peter Smith's high school graduation picture and
yearbook. South High School, Denver, Colorado, 1956. The background
scenery is Middle Mountain, West Virginia, where, many years later, Pete
liked to ride his horse Unique.

Monday Creek Publishing | P.O. Box 399 | Buchtel, Ohio USA
mondaycreekpublishing.com

1. Smith, Aboott P. 2. Veterinarians – Ohio – Athens 3. Cowboy – Rodeo
– Colorado   4. Essays

ISBN-10: 0692864520
ISBN-13: 978-0692864524

For
Jody, Jessica, and Pat

Special thanks to Colorado South High School Alumni, to friends old and new who continue to support and nurture the legacy of Peter Smith.

Foreword

Nestled between dusty pictures, hallowed keepsakes, and worn letters, Peter Smith kept his high school essays neatly bundled in a leather zippered notebook. Among the essays are pages of trig homework, book reports, and random musings. Most of the essays are handwritten, some marked with red, indicating a correction or praise by Peter's writing teacher. Each essay has a remark by the teacher, usually affirmation of Peter's prolific writing skills. *"Excellent material, Peter."*

Born and raised on the Maine coast, Peter learned early the love of animals, the joy of art, literature, and the benefits of hard work. Moving to Colorado with his family as a young teen would bring Peter into manhood. When he was fourteen, his parents returned to the east, leaving Peter behind to live his cowboy dream.

A talented and passionate student, Peter is remembered by his South High classmates as an "enjoyable fellow." Writing for the Senate Club and the Writer's Bureau, Peter's essays are true to his cowboy lifestyle, while others are tongue-in-cheek. After graduating high school in 1956, Peter enrolled in college. In 1962, Dr. Abbott "Pete" Smith, graduated from Colorado State University. He was, and remains, well known as a skilled surgeon and veterinarian.

Along with memories from Peter's High School Yearbook, we present to you a teen who was a fan of Winston Churchill, enjoyed writing, academia, and, most of all, loved living the life of a cowboy.

Gina McKnight

Contents

Another Horse to Break

I sat on the top pole of the weatherbeaten corral contemplating the four-year-old sorrel stallion which was standing by the far wall.

"He sure is a beauty, isn't he Burl?" I said more than asked.

"He's all right," was the reply, "he'll make a good horse once he's gentled down."

There was silence again as Burl took a sack of Bull Durham from his left shirt pocket. He opened the sack with his teeth, a thumb, and a forefinger. Taking a cigarette paper from the side of the sack, he held it between his thumb and forefinger and made a trough into which he poured a little pile of dry brown tobacco. He pulled the drawstrings shut and put the sack back in his pocket. The lithe muscular fingers smoothed out the stuff, and with a rolling motion of thumbs and forefingers he enveloped it in the fine white paper. He licked the cigarette along the seam and twisting one end put the other between his lips.

Lighting a match on his Levis, he held it cupped in his tanned and calloused hands while he lit his cigarette; then rubbing the burned out match with his fingers, he held it by the tip and dropped it into the dirt.

"You know what I'd like to see?"

"No, what?"

"A wild horseshoeing contest."

"That's about the only thing they didn't have at Cheyenne this year."

We looked again at the horse. He sure was a dandy.

"What do you say we do it like they do in the wild horse racing at Cheyenne?"

"All right by me; let's go."

I took my nylon rope and started walking.

"I'll squeeze him past you along the fence," Burl volunteered.

"All right, I'll catch him and let him pull me around till you get there. Then we can work up to him along the rope, and - well, no need making any long range plans, I guess."

Burl went around him, and the horse started past me along the fence. I caught him and held on. Burl got there, and together we worked up to him along the thirty-three feet of rope. We finally got to his head.

"You want to mug him while I go get the saddle?" I asked.

"O.K."

I held the rope while Burl clamped on to the poor critter's head with the vice-like grip of a bulldogger and sank his teeth into the horse's right ear.

The saddle, bridle, and blanket were huddled in the corner. I got them and went back to Burl and the horse.

Throwing the sheepskin blanket on, I cinched up the saddle and took the rope.

"You can let go of Reddy's ear now if you want to," I said.

He did.

I forced the horse's jaws, slipped in the snaffle bit, and adjusted the bridle while Burl held the rope. It was a beat-up old bridle with no jowl strap or even a curb. Somehow I was really attached to the old thing though. It was just right for the job since I didn't have a hackamore. Couldn't hurt his mouth with some accidental sharp pull like if you were using a spade bit. Still you could discipline him.

Gripping the reins beneath his quivering lower lip, I gave a last look at the rigging.

I passed the right rein over his neck, and pulling his head to the left, I mounted him easily and confidently. It seemed strange to me how I was always nervous while fooling around with a horse that I knew was going to buck. Once I was on him the feeling disappeared and everything in me solidified; my whole system settled down. It felt good up there.

Automatically I took a deep seat and swinging my stirrups slightly forward leaned just a little bit back; then as I took a long rein, he felt the slack and started giving me everything he had.

Explaining how I feel when I'm riding a bucking horse is hard. There's an odd sensation of knowing the horse is bucking, but there's no real feeling to it. It's like fighting, in that I'm kind of numb through the rest of the fight after the first wallop.

As the horse bucked I suddenly began to feel off balance. The horse felt it too, and with a sudden burst of earnest bucking he unloaded me solidly into the corral fence. I wonder what it would be like to fly. I was probably in the air long enough to find out.

Had the horse been one of the stock buckers we kept

around for rodeo purposes I would have felt like calling it a day, but you can't do that when you're breaking a horse. If you're still whole you've got to get back on and ride him out. The worst thing I could have done would have been to let the son of a gun think that he had accomplished something by throwing me.

It was for these reasons that I gathered myself from the fence and ambled over to the horse. I happened to glance at Burl just then. He was meditating over a spot on his hand with as straight a face as you'd hope to see.

I managed to corner the horse and taking the reins, I again mounted him. He shied badly as I got on, and for a minute I thought I was done for, but somehow I stayed with him. For what seemed like a long time he tossed and turned, bucked, crow hopped, and bucked again, never sparing me a second's rest.

Bucking is hard on a horse though; it jars his every bone, raises havoc with his joints, and pulls his muscles besides taking a lot of energy. A good minute of that is approximately equal to a good day's work.

Four minutes of hard amateur bucking and this horse was through. He stopped, and in short, jumpy steps started walking.

"I like this life. I like to feel the splash of cold water against my face in the morning and the feel of the blankets of my unmade bed at night."

Peter Smith

Benny

*B*enny is the school janitor. He works full-time and a little extra from seven-thirty in the morning till after six at night. No one knows he's there, seems like, or sees him, but me. I'm the mouse that supervises the inner workings of the place, while Benny polishes the floors and does all the little chores that janitors do.

If I were one of these humans, there's nobody I'd rather have for a friend than old Ben. I really like him, but there's not much that I can do to show it except keep the holes small and not leave crumbs around. Benny knows that I love him, though, and I'm sure that he loves me and appreciates the little things I do.

Benjamin, that's Benny's real name, usually whistles while he works; but lately he started singing. He's got a voice that's pretty clear for a man his age. Just a few days ago, he crackled into a Christmas Carol, and he's been singing Carols ever since. I can tell that he's really happy. Actually, I don't suppose that he's got too much to be happy about, the way most people think of happiness. He's getting old and tired, all except for his heart, which must be growing bigger every day. He lives in a little room in the basement way in back of the furnace. That room is always as shiny as the new penny I found in front of the hole in Room 215. Ben doesn't have any relations either, as far as I can tell. It almost seems as though nobody in the world loves old Ben anymore, but me.

Benny never seems to get tired of his job, and he's always trying to do it better. He does all the little things that nobody ever notices, like lifting up the table legs when he sweeps and sweeping the corners extra carefully. He doesn't shove the chairs around, but picks them up and sets them down as if each one were a part of him. When he's all through with a room, he likes to look back, and a smile that cuts into me always comes to his wrinkled face. Then he flicks off the light and shuffles to the next room.

He isn't always happy, though; sometimes he sits down at one of the little desks and tears come to his eyes. I feel like running out of my hole and jumping up into his lap and cuddling under his whiskery chin, but there's always a little bit too much mouse in me.

Best of all, Ben likes to sweep the big auditorium. I can tell, because he always sings louder when he's working there. He loves to walk down the aisles or between the rows.

He's always a little shy about sweeping the stage and doesn't sing then. Once he did just a kind of dance step, then stopped and finished quickly. Lots of times when there's a set on the stage he'll stand looking at it. Maybe he can see actors dancing and singing as I do. I wish Benny would run onto the stage and sing and dance sometime. I know he could do it real well if he'd try. I'm a pretty good actor myself, and if it's good and dark, sometimes I go out there and do a number, provided there aren't any other mice around. Of course, I'm so little that I can't do much, but it's fun to try stuff. Just to run out onto the stage from under a curtain and then jump into the air is fun. I'm trying to get up enough nerve to do a somersault in midair, but I haven't so far.

Christmas assembly was yesterday. Christmas must be just around the corner. Everybody knows when Christmas comes, but it's funny to me in a way that people should celebrate the day that the great white mouse was born so very long ago. Maybe something happened for the humans the same day, and that's why they celebrate it. Whatever the reason is, it's fine by me; it makes people happy, and I like to see people happy.

I wonder what Benny's going to do. He won't get any presents from anyone, because there just isn't anyone to send him a present. Maybe he'll go to church and get whatever he can in love and warmth there, but he doesn't have anything to wear to church, and he's so shy that he probably won't go. If only someone would go to him and be to him what my wife Matilda is to me, it would sure make me happy; but, like I said, he's got no relatives, and he doesn't have any girlfriends. If there were only something that I could do...I've got it! I'll give him my new penny!

Pete,
Good luck and best wishes always to a real great guy. I hope that our friendship, which has developed in the past three years, will continue to prosper.

Good luck always,
Jim Morgan
Sr. Class President
High School Yearbook

Pete,

Well, this year is finally over and it's really been great, agreed? The sports section is really fabulous and I think you're to be commended for your job as sports editor. Best of luck at Aggies, I know you'll do great. This summer should prove to be very interesting for you.

See you in the future,
George
High School Yearbook

Spy for a Night

I had been working for Mr. Roth the weekend of the tenth, exercising his horses, chopping wood, and doing other odd jobs. I was to go back this weekend for more work, but there were complications. In the first place I was without transportation, for my father had the car, and the busses didn't come within fifteen miles of Mr. Roth's place.

Feeling energetic and ambitious, I decided upon a plan of attack. I would take the '8' downtown, transfer to the '28' which would get me to Lakeside, and I would walk from there. Leaving home at six-thirty, I should be able to make it by one o'clock and catch a wink or two before starting work in the morning.

The first part of the trip went like clockwork, except for an hour wait for the '28' and before long I reached Lakeside. There I got off the bus and started walking north toward Arvada. I went a few hundred yards before I decided that it might pay to hitch a ride. Rather than walk with my thumb out, I stood beneath a streetlight where prospective ride-donors could see me in all my shining innocence. I waited a little over an hour before I was offered a ride, which took me to the edge of Arvada at Fifty-third and Wadsworth. I decided to walk from there, and went at a walk-trot to Eightieth and Wadsworth, where I asked directions as to the Roth residence. I was directed northward, though I found later that at that very spot I had been about two miles east of ground zero. I started north, thumbing as I went, and soon got a ride with two boys from California. They clipped along, and almost before I knew what was happening I was in Broomfield. The two boys let me out there, and I walked westward down the highway to the Denver-Boulder Turnpike tollhouse, where I asked directions again. I guess I'll never learn not to ask directions. The cop told me that there was an old dirt road going east from there that might take me a little closer to where I wanted to go. He didn't know just where it went, and

I had no idea at all, but I was willing to try anything.

By the time I hit the dirt road I had been traveling over five hours, and I was getting tired. I tried to lie down and sleep till morning, when I figured that my sense of direction would return to me as I saw the mountains in the west. I walked over to a tangled barbed-wire fence and lay down. I quickly jumped up with a seat-full of stickers. It isn't every day that prickly pears and yucca bushes get to play host to such a willing guest. After a bit of reconnoitering at the cost of a couple more handfuls of stickers (it was a dark, moonless night), I found a place where I could lie down on bare ground. It was a fairly warm night, and I thought I would be able to sleep, but I found that the cold earth soon sucked the heat from my body and left me shivering.

I walked until my body heat was restored and then tried again with the same result, except that I found I could not stay lying down as long as before. I tried the same thing three or four more times before coming to the realization that I would have to keep walking till morning to keep warm. The idea did not particularly appeal to me, as I did not know where I was going, and it was still a long time until dawn.

This country which I was passing through was desolate. I had not seen even a farmhouse or a tree. The little dirt road kept going and going. Turning off to the left at each "intersection," I found that the trail began to grow fainter and fainter as I followed it toward what I judged from all the lights to be a small town. It seemed odd that the trail should dwindle upon approaching such a thriving metropolis. At any rate it was pleasing to know that warmth and shelter were in sight. Seeing that colony of lights only a matter of a few miles away was like coming upon a nice big cool snowbank in the southern regions of Hell. It looked great!

The lights disappeared for about two hours as I walked down into and across a huge basin through which coursed a number of gullies of various sizes. Near the bottom of the basin I came upon the first tree that I had seen since leaving the tollhouse on the turnpike – that wonderful, warm, friendly little place! How I wished now that I had stayed there and accepted the patrolman's offer of a ride back to Denver when he got off duty and went home. I couldn't think of turning back at the time though – not me. I had to keep making mistakes – never would learn when to quit.

There was a little bit of grass that closed off the cold of the ground slightly. I layed down and tried desperately to sleep. I still couldn't. I started climbing out of the basin and finally made my way back to the "surface." I saw the lights as I came over the top, but something puzzled me and I stopped and looked. The lights weren't scattered around. They were arranged in circles and squares and rows. Coming closer, I could see that the lights and buildings were all enclosed in a fifteen-foot steel mesh fence with four strands of barbed wire at the top. I began a tour of my own around the outside of the fence, noticing the red and white U.S. PROPERTY signs. Inside the fence was a blacktop road which ran right along the barrier. In a few minutes a tan Ford pickup came driving around the inside. I waved my arms at the men in the truck, but they drove on by. I whistled at them, and they screeched to a stop and then backed up.

"Could you tell me where I am?"

"Come on up to the gate."

I trotted slowly up to the gate about one hundred yards away. By the time I got there someone had radioed two other pickups. I could distinguish three letters: A., E., and C. I finally knew where I was. Upon their arrival, along with that of a sedan, I was admitted into the sacred precincts of Rocky Flats.

"Do you know that you are on Federal Property?"

"I do now."

"These men will take you to headquarters."

I was placed in the backseat of the sedan between two armed guards. In a few moments we reached "headquarters," a small office building at the end of a loosely strung corridor of men looking at the car which held the "spy."

The men ushered me inside the building, where the captain showed me a chair and questioned me daintily but exhaustively.

"What is your father's full name? Your mother's" Do you have any brothers and sisters? How old are they? What are their full names? Where do they go to school? How did you get here? Where were you going? Who do you work for? What does he do? Who does your father work for? What does he do? Where were you born? Your mom? Your dad? Your brothers and sisters?" Anything of importance of anything that resembled a question in any way was put to me.

"Anything you want to tell me?"

I didn't say the things that I wanted to. He already knew my life history, and I'm not even through growing yet!

"No."

"I think you're all right, but there's one more man I'd like for you to talk to before you go."

The Admiral was phoned, and an hour or so later he arrived, talked to the captain, and took me into his office. He showed me his F.B.I. card and told me his name (which escapes me at the moment). He then proceeded to ask me the exact questions that the captain had and added a few of his own. I think that I detected a shade of disappointment in his countenance when he could not find any incongruities in the two lists of answers after he returned from another talk with the captain.

Twelve and a half hours after I had left home I was escorted in the pickup, still seated between armed guards, to work. My career as a potentially destructive spy had been ruthlessly shattered.

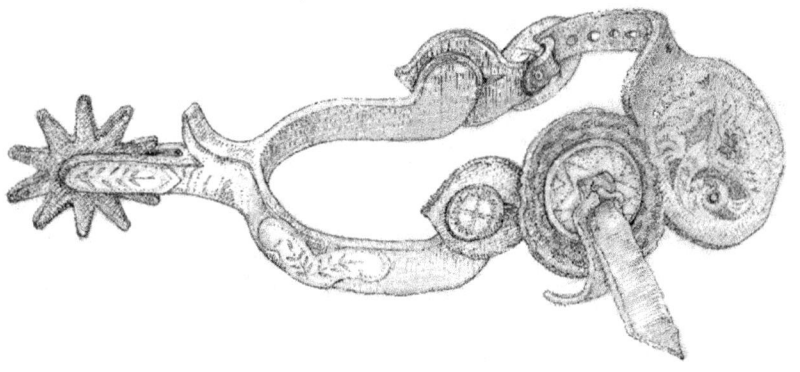

Opening Day

$\mathcal{F}$our miles west of Buffalo, Colorado, a small town situated near the North Fork of the South Platte and Buffalo Creek is a small, rough cabin. This cabin lies in the heart of some of the most beautiful country in Colorado. This is Pike National Forest where the trout leap from the rapids and the placid waters of the beaver dams. Deer and other animals large and small roam here and there under the lofty pines and firs. Mountain sheep range above timberline in a paradise all their own. Suddenly the dams begin to ripple for another reason;

this wilderness wonderland has been invaded by fishermen young and old in search of the world famous Rocky Mountain trout.

I am not immune to the lure of a good day of fishing; so with my equipment consisting of pole, line, and a few hooks, I set out to try my luck. There are no good fishing holes in front of the cabin, but as I think back I recall a fishing hole worthy of the name, and it is there that I go. Early morning in the mountains is very cold, but that does not bother the fish, and the first cast nets a fine large rainbow. The second fish was also a beauty, but the morning was becoming warm and light. There were other pools which I wanted to fish up the stream; so I went up the stream with high hopes of catching my limit before noon. This did not prove to be the case with us, and after a light lunch we drove up the road following the upward course of the stream until a fork in the creek was reached. I took the left branch and in a few minutes I was to find that I had caught my limit.

The day had been a very profitable one. Twenty-eight fish had been caught by four of us. We could easily have caught as many more if time and limits had permitted, but one of our number had an appointment in Denver which necessarily had to be kept. With full hearts and reels we turned homeward from this enchanting place to slip quietly under a smoky blanket into the bustling and busy city of Denver.

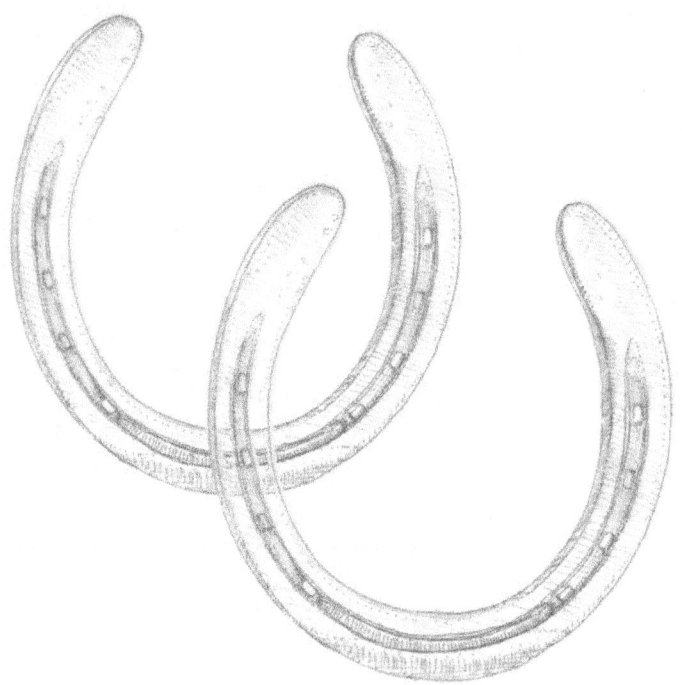

The Day the Horses Got Out

$\mathcal{I}$ got up early that morning to wrangle some horses. We were going to drive a small herd over the ridge from the flats, and the two horses we had in were tired and getting sore-footed. Our horse pasture was a good one. It covered six sections of flat, rolling plain land and was all newly fenced on the north, south, east, and west. I was trotting slowly and waiting for the sun to rise. I ought to have them in before the sun came up.

The sun had risen when I got back to the home corrals without any horses. Some city dude in a cream-colored '53

Merc. had been through the ranch earlier with his wife and a carload of kids. I suppose they were the culprits. I didn't think to take his license number as I usually do a strange car. He had on a Stetson, and I thought he was some rancher going the long way to Horse Creek. At any rate he had left the gate open.

Dee and I did the chores. After breakfast we saddled up and rode to the foot of the ridge. We couldn't see any horses.

They were halfway up the ridge feeding on a rim of one of the larger canyons. We made our way carefully around. When we were above them we started walking our horses slowly in their direction. They wouldn't walk; they had to run. We had tired horses and did not try to head them off toward the gate. The little bunch of sorrels, browns, and blacks was really dusting along down the ridge to the west. Eventually they would reach the flats. It would be about four miles from the foot of the ridge to the gate. The bunch reached the flats in less than five minutes; we took about fifteen.

We decided to follow over to the west fence and push them two miles south through the gate.

They didn't stop at the windmill, but kept right on going until they got to the fence. Everything was going fine. They'd move south now and through the gate. Dee and I would still be able to drive those cows if nothing went wrong.

Then it happened. About fifty antelope came clipping along from the east back towards the ridge. I don't know where a bunch that size came from in June, but there they were. Those darn fool horses just had to chase them too, and there was nothing we could do to stop them. The antelope kept running all the way to the foot of the ridge with the horses behind them. They then turned north, but the horses kept on going right up the ridge.

Oh well, those cows could wait another day.

We slowed our sweating horses to a trot and then a walk. It would take quite a while to get that bunch now.

It was getting along toward noon when we topped the ridge. We'd really have to catch the day by the tail to get anything done. We had two horses in a pasture at the old King place that hadn't done anything all summer because of cuts. They should be all right by this time, I figured. Since my horse was beginning to limp slightly and Dee's was also pooped out, we decided to run them into the old sheep corral there. We got them in, changed, and turned ours into the pasture. The new horses bucked when we got on, but by the time we were back to where we thought the horses were, they were getting tired. They were fat and soft from their easy summer.

The wayward herd apparently saw us before we saw them. They were headed up the east side of the ridge. We spotted them high above us from the hollow under the lip of the ridge.

Dee and I split up. I followed the horses to the left, and he went up the ridge farther to the right.

When I got to the top of the ridge, the horses were nowhere in sight. They were probably headed down toward the flats. I'd have to make tracks if I was going to catch them now, for it was almost sundown. I started down the ridge to the right and joined Dee after a few miles. We went part of the way together.

Once we caught a glimpse of them dipping into a ravine, and we watched as they climbed the other side.

We split up again. This time I went to the right and Dee went left. The sun was gone.

Down one canyon, follow it a way, then up, over, and down another. Once, going through a stand of trees on an old trail, I felt an odd sensation. I happened to look back to see a bobcat and a lynx as they crossed the trail hunting. It was the first time I had ever seen that. From then on, I picked my way carefully.

Now and then as I rode along a ridge I would see the horses. They were black objects gliding along a ridge, a cloud of silvery dust streaming out behind them as they ran. Then, as they plunged into the pitch darkness near the flats I lost them and didn't see them again. I couldn't figure out why they were still running like that. They all had a little mustang blood in them; maybe that was what did it.

I got to the flats a little before Dee. He whistled, and we got together.

One day all shot because of a city dude.

Well, we'd try again in the morning.

Pete,
I've enjoyed working with you a great deal during the past year, both on the annual and in the Senate Club.

Good luck to you,
Mr. Robert W. Larson, A.B., M.A.
Social Science
High School Yearbook

The Master Mind

Positive thinking along a few lines
Can make for a life that will pay
To you and mankind in many a way.
Aim for a definite goal – no matter how high!
Don't place a limit – not even the sky!
Look forward to failures – make them count as successes.
He that succeeds ne'er to failure confesses!
Make a habit of saving and accurate thought;
With imagination great things can be wrought;
With self-control and confidence
Pierce the forests of doubt, no matter how dense.
Do more than you're paid for and concentrate;
A personality pleasing will open many a gate.
Take the initiative with a leader's drive;
Toward tolerance and co-operation always strive.
Do all this by The Golden Rule
And you will find
That you can tool
The Master Mind!

"He came out of the gate just bubbling with ambition, but when he saw all those people he just stood stock still. I was so polluted that I fell off anyway."

Peter Smith

Rodeo

The Saturday of the Arlington Rodeo was here. Frank had let the other fellows and me off work. Jim went into town and got two cases of beer. A rodeo day can put an awful big dent in a pile of beer cans. We threw my bareback riggings and Dee's bronc saddle into the trunk, put the beer between us on the front seat, and took off for Arlington.

The '51 Ford got us there long before noon, and we went to Pop Worth's shack. He was glad to see us; said he thought people had forgotten how to knock with their elbows. We told him where we were going to park and invited him to come up and see us after a while, when the beer was really cold.

There was an old tub resting peacefully against the woodshed. In about fifteen minutes it was a couple hundred yards up the creek and resting on the bottom, plumb full with beer cans. It didn't take much for them to get good and cold, and before long that old 3.2 plus 3 was flowing like water. The rodeo didn't begin till one. We just sat around, talking, smoking, and quenching our growing thirsts.

Before long a couple of the Rock Springs boys that I'd met on another ranch up there showed up. They were Burl, Greenall, Hanks, and Ed. They all had gals with them. There were some big doings at Elk Mountain after the rodeo. Louie Armstrong was playing. I don't know how they ever got him to play there, but he sure did. That was what my old friends had come down for. The rodeo was only a sidelight. They had plenty of booze with them. We talked about old times until nearly one-thirty; then Dee and I and a couple of the other fellows waded down the creek, laughing and pushing each other into the water.

When we got to the corrals the rodeo was just beginning. They never start on time. I was pretty well sobered up from the cold water. I needed more beer. They'll sell beer to anybody that's big enough to hold a can at those small rodeos.

I watched some of the events. The calf roping came first.

The ropers had a rough time of it. The people were crowded around the chutes, and the arena was so small that the calf hardly reached the other end before he was coming back. It seemed as though a roper wouldn't be able to catch his calf without knocking somebody's hat off. None of the men cared though; they weren't after money, just a good time.

Next, they had the kids colt riding. It was the first one they'd ever had at Arlington. The horses were just as scared as the kids riding them and green as grass. They couldn't buck worth a hoot, but the kids all fell off two jumps out of the gate anyway, and everybody laughed. Then there was bull dogging and team roping.

Finally came saddle bronc riding. Dee's horse broke from the chute at a full lope. He kept going right out into the middle of the arena. Then, *baloom*! The horse went straight up and came down a long time before Dee landed - and I mean landed! The broncs weren't professional, but had a little natural talent. They were Jimmy Mann's hay horses, getting their kinks out before the season began.

Next came the bareback horses. Bull riding usually followed the saddle broncs, but the bulls had started fighting, knocked the fence down, and got away. I later heard from Pop Worth that it had taken some good cowboys almost a week to get the critters corralled again. The fellows helped me cinch up the surcingle. We flanked him and waited. I watched the others go. Gates one, two, and three opened, and then out I went on Dynamite. Yes, sir, he was real dynamite. He came out of the gate just bubbling with ambition, but when he saw all those people he just stood stock still. I was so polluted that I fell off anyway, landing like a wet rag. I got up unhurt. Wet rags never do get hurt. I walked dazedly over to the fence, and sat down between Bill and Dee, who were heartily partaking of ye old beverage.

I didn't see much of those last events. Cow riding and working – horse contests I guess they were, but it was a real fine rodeo, yessir, a mighty fine rodeo.

Religion

$\mathcal{R}$eligion is important in varying degrees, to the lives of approximately 2,074,608,195 people in the world today. There are many types of religions, Christian and non-Christian which in most cases have been tailor-made to fit the needs of the people. This has taken years of doing and to a certain extent the process is still being carried on in all of them as civilization advances and new needs arise. The constant separation and splitting up in the Christian Churches, to give a specific example, is certainly symptomatic of this. The Baptists, Methodists, etc. etc. are some of the more "recent"

breakings while the later breakings are practically innumerable. This will be happening as long as there are living religions.

Many a man's life would be incomplete in almost every phase were he not able to turn to a faultless something bigger than himself; something to trust and lean back on when everything else seems to have collapsed. Even the most primitive peoples sensed this; and if a god of some kind was not handed down to them or if the number of their gods proved insufficient they found it necessary to invent a few or to endow the old ones with greater capabilities and powers. The more ignorant the people the greater is the degree of superstition and hence the greater the number of gods. If a man had no knowledge of the natural elements which caused rain or even an idea thereof he invented a rain god, no understanding of fire at all and a fire god resulted and etc. But as a people advances and attains greater scientific enlightenment fewer gods become necessary until finally, monotheism results in most cases. When a man understands what causes rain and that there is nothing that will put the water cycle from its course, he needs no rain god; with an understanding of fire; a fire god is no longer a necessity and so on.

Why is the final state of monotheism still necessary? Why and when do men turn to a God. The answer may differ with the personality but usually it is when they are confronted with an "unexplainable" problem, poverty in the sense of physical need, or a method of elucidation of an idea, theory, or whatever when human calculations fail to produce an answer. When and if physical needs no longer press, death to the individual or even his loved ones is no longer feared; problems, theories, questions have all been answered and set down on paper with flawless scientific accuracy through ever progressing science, what will be the need of a god? What will happen when physical comfort is carried to the final extreme, fear of anything is unknown, and people find themselves stagnant and entirely lacking in the initiative to search out greater things?

Scientific enlightenment, however, doesn't seem to produce stagnancy of the *mind*. Each great discovery leads to another in a seemingly infinite series. The developmental atomic power, for instance, has raised many more questions than it has answered in the threat of actual absolute demolition or at any rate a drastic and terrifying retarding and setting back of civilization in a final world war. Can science explain the original source of energy, duplicate photosynthesis, or explain electricity? These are but a very few of the many things which science finds itself incapable of explaining. There are still many things for which something infinitely big must be turned to, to blame and explain. Will death ever be eliminated and speculations to life after death be discontinued?

The Conquest of Old Scraggy

The teachers' convention had come at last, giving both teachers and their opponents a chance for some much-needed relaxation. Sam, a classmate of mine, and I had decided to spend that long weekend camping in Pike National Forest.

Sam's folks took us up there early Thursday morning and left us on a side road. We made our way with grub, sleeping bags, and other unneeded boy scout type camping accessories to a spot near Turtle Creek. This brimming river is about a foot and three inches wide and lies between Green Mountain and

Old Scraggy.

All day Thursday we did nothing but set up what we called a camp and fool around. There was some free iron in the creek, so we panned for several hours and got enough to make two knife blades – when smeltered – and perhaps a small nail to boot.

Our "camp" consisted of some sadistic-looking boulders for a shelter, sleeping bags, a beautiful stone fireplace, smoothly constructed in a matter of minutes, and nearly ten pounds of the wrong things to eat. The fireplace was built a few feet ahead of the sleeping bags, so that we could stoke it from our goodly pile of squaw wood without leaving our sleeping bags.

It was colder that night than my fondest expectations. Every time I turned over, cold air could suck in around me and then rush out past me, leaving my teeth jangling tightly in my head in spite of the bravely smoldering fire nearby. Finally, I got to sleep, letting the fire go out. That was a poor trade, because a second and a half later I woke up again. I found, upon peeking daringly from my sleeping bag, that icy-fingered dawn had come in all its rosy glory. Sam was sleeping soundly – the rat. I took a paper sack that was shielding some cowardly potatoes. Dumping the spuds the sack lay down in the teepee I built and was greedily gobbled by a match.

Awakening at short – too short – intervals, I added wood

to the cheery blaze, until after some two or three hours it was safe to venture forth from my shell.

There was an inch of ice in the kettle. This gradually "melted" until the pot became so warm that I could pour it without my fingertips sticking. Sam woke up – after it had become pleasantly warm – to announce from his luxuriant eider-down nest that last night hadn't been so cold after all. I would have thrown him into the creek if it had been big enough and unfrozen.

A breakfast of coffee, bacon, and pancakes helped soothe the aching ulcers, and we started contemplating the conquest of Old Scraggy. We made plans and packed the knapsack until dear old Sol was smiling beneficently upon some sheltering black clouds in the near southeast. Ah, the thrill of mountain climbing! To get deliciously cold and superbly tired once again.

We chose the gentlest side, for we had a long way to go. The mountain was snow-splotched and steep. Old Scraggy looked better from a distance. We trudged, pulled, and pushed up the mountain, working the process to scientific perfection. Sam would lead one hundred steps; then we'd change, and I'd lead a hundred. Onward ho! Lead on to something and someplace that I don't particularly care to be.

Several hours later, we stopped and built a fire on a jutting rock and enjoyed a scenic broadside view of a neighboring mole hill. Saturated with the intense beauty thereof, I lay down on the coldest rock west of the Mississippi and dozed peacefully for about a minute. Sam had brought along his Rye-Krisps and peanut butter. Together with some cheese and raisins, these made a perfectly exquisite meal.

We couldn't stop then; we had to see what kind of rock the top of the mountain was made of. One hundred paces – stop - change – I lead 75 – change stop – Sam leads 50. Where is the top anyway! Every step requires a tremendous amount of energy now, for we must be approaching sea level. The air is thin up here. We fight valiantly onward. The top is in sight. Up, up and over! This pile of rocks should be called Old Tabletop. We keep climbing ever upward. There's the top for sure. A final surge of lung-tearing, muscle rending effort brings us to the top. The view is magnificent. All around, and looking down upon us, rise majestic towering monuments of granite. This view has never before been experienced, I am sure. Walking among the boulders at the top of the highest part of this mountain, we kick away the beer cans, as we came to the final towering pinnacle. Upon this there is a circular bronze plaque reading "elevation 9,000 feet." Sam and I rolled a couple boulders over the edge in the old tradition; then we started down.

We couldn't get off that mountain fast enough. Over boulders, under boulders, around boulders, and in and out of caves and tunnels of boulders. Many a time on the way down did we stop to enjoy the scenic view of...boulders. When we hit the bottom of the mountain, we ran nearly all the way back to camp.

I felt a burning inside me after supper that night. A burning deep in the pit of my stomach. Too much pepper on those potatoes.

Pete,
Good luck at A&M. I know you'll go a long way and become a big cattle king. Then we'll build a ski-area of our own and go skiing every day.

Dick Thomas
Fellow student
High School Yearbook

Poachers

We were plumb out of meat. We didn't usually eat beef, because it's hard enough to clean up a profit in the ranching business anyway without eating up the beef critters yourself. Hank and I have slaughtered a lame two-year-old bull, but he was tougher'n flint, and you couldn't hardly cut even the steaks with an ordinary knife.

After chores I took my most prized possession, a Winchester 22 from the bunkhouse wall and put it in the cab of the Willy's pickup. A 22. doesn't pack the power of the bigger guns, but then it doesn't make much noise. I saddled up Badger, loaded him in (the pickup was equipped with a stock rack), and off we went.

Hank and I moved the small truck across the flats toward the ridge at a good rate, kicking up the little cloud of dust that follows a fellow everywhere in the plain country.

After a gate and two cattle guards, we were at the foot of the ridge that lay about ten miles from the home place. Hank slammed the tin lizzy into four-wheel drive when we started climbing. She managed to make it up the hill to the reservoir. Badger rode good in the pickup. The bumps didn't bother him. A few times I think he kept the old jeep from turning over by leaning in the right direction. I wouldn't want to take any other horse that I knew of over a road like that.

We unloaded Badger at the reservoir, which was just a dam holding back a mud puddle in one of the bigger canyons. I put my rifle into the scabbard hanging from the saddle and started off. Hank drove the jeep into a thick clump of trees and waited for me. I like to hunt from a horse.

I walked Badger into the wind diagonally across the canyons till we came to the top. There were usually a couple of deer in a pocket under the cliffs near the old sheep pillar. I tied up Badger and walked up to a place where there was a split in the ridge. I slipped down the deep, wide crack to a rim where the ridge leveled off, then dropped again near a cottonwood grove. Sure enough, when I reached the bottom and rounded some large boulders, there were two fat spikes. This was better luck than I expected. The biggest one grazed into a perfect position. I plastered him behind the shoulder, and he dropped as if he'd been hit by a pile driver. With the knife that Pa gave me last Christmas, I dressed him out and packed him back to the horse. The 22. hollowpoint had smashed his heart. Badger was an old hand at this, though he was only five years old, and the smell didn't bother him the way it does some horses. I broke him of that by smearing rabbit blood on his nose. Putting the rifle back in the scabbard, I got on and rode back to the truck.

Hank and I put the buck on the floor of the cab under some gunny sacks, just in case, loaded the horse again, and started down the ridge. We kept the lights off, because the hunting season wasn't too far off, and game wardens were always thick this time of the year. They seemed to travel in or on almost anything that walked, crawled, or flew. I didn't see how we could have missed one; for when we hit the foot of the ridge and were started along the road home, I looked back and saw the flash of car lights as a car of some kind or other traveled slowly along near the top of the ridge. Maybe someday those boys will wise up and learn to travel with their lights off.

It was dark, and coming down the ridge we could see car lights playing back and forth across the flats. Poachers! Never turning our lights on, we kept going to the barns and unloaded and fed my horse. In the far end of an old sheep shed were some meat hooks, where we always hung our deer. We leisurely skinned out the deer by the light of a kerosene lamp and even took time to tack out the hide on the wall with some other skins in a dark corner of the shed behind some piled-up gunny sacks and barrels. Most of the poachers that I know don't save the hides because of the risk, but I've always been willing to take the chance.

After giving the warden on the ridge plenty of time to move on, we hopped into the jeep and started out to pick up some tricks of the trade.

It was hard driving down the road from the ranch. The night had become pitch dark. With my lights off I swayed down the road. All that I could see were faint whitish streaks, and I couldn't see them most of the time. The road had been made dangerously near the fence, so that I had a hard time keeping from running into it.

After traveling about three or four miles east, I slowed down and went through a gate into a steer pasture to begin my poacher poaching. We moved another quarter mile forward; suddenly headlights came over the top of our jeep. I thought the game was over then, but the hunters didn't see us. We crept closer and closer. Just as they caught several antelope in their lights and started chasing them, scaring the scattered steers, we turned on our lights.

The car started southwest when they saw us, but we let them go. There was a big ditch running northwest not too far ahead. The jalopy that those boys were driving wouldn't be able to make it, unless it had the engine of a tank. We plowed along with our lights off, until the car ahead came to the ditch. Then we turned on our lights again and started towards it. The poachers outmoved us – with a little goodwill on our part – and headed back north along the fence. We bounced after them with our lights off. They turned theirs off too but in a few minutes had them on again. This country wasn't easy on anyone who didn't know it. We wouldn't have had ours off if we didn't think we knew the country pretty well. I knew this ranch like the palm of my...whoosh! The jeep dipped down hard. I didn't move but my stomach did, and my heart wasn't crowding my Adam's apple because I was afraid that the jeep would get smashed either. We came up again quickly, though, and my stomach slapped back into place. I began to think how happy I was that there was only one dip like that on the place, thunk! The same thing happened again. It wasn't the kind of thing that gives a real thrill when you're forty. I snapped on the lights and swerved around a steer just in time. The good Lord must have been watching over me, that I hadn't hit any before. We cramped the boys in against the fence, and finally they stopped.

"What're you hunting?"

"Rabbits."

A buck-toothed kid held up a squash-headed rabbit.

"You're sure about that, are you?"

That feller was really scared. You could tell, and that old bluffer Hank wasn't helping the driver any by inspecting the bridge of his nose over the sights.

"Sssure."

"All right, we just wondered; you see there's been a lot of poaching going on around here lately. Why, we've had to shoot up a couple of guys already."

"By the way, where's your rabbit license?"

"Well, then, I guess we'll have to turn you three guys in. Drive up a ways so we can get a good look at your license plate."

They drove up all right, but I don't know how far they went before they stopped.

Hank and I laughed all the way home.

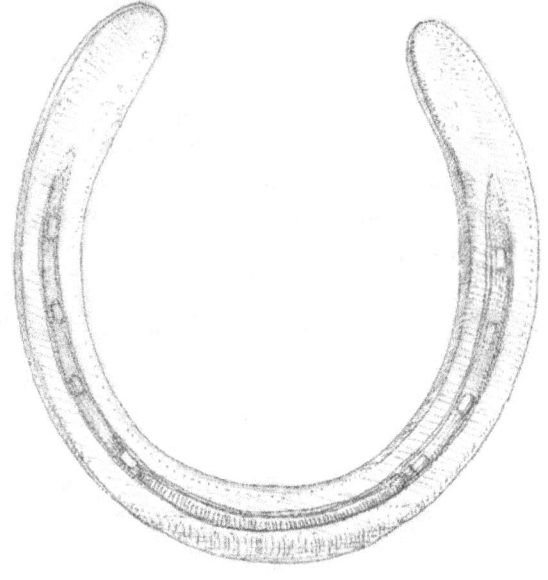

Pete,

It's really been great knowing you this year. I believe we have formed a real friendship. I, too, hope that in future years we may meet again. We have a lot in common, Best of everything to a sincerely great fellow.

Wes
Annual Staff/Fellow Student
High School Yearbook

Cowpoke

What keeps a cowboy on the job? The pay? That isn't likely. The work is as tough as work comes, and the day is usually one hundred bucks a month or less. Insurance of a steady job? No, cowboying is as unsteady a job as you'll find. You work through the summer; then you may stay on through the winter, but there's not enough work for all of the hands. Steady year-round work is hard to find. Is it because the cowboy can't get a "better" job with which he can at least be sure of pay and a piece of ground to be buried in! No, that's not it either. Most any cowpoke I know of could get a job that paid two or three times what he gets. It's hard to put the answer into any other words than "because I like it."

I like it from the black hours before dawn to the equally black hours after sunset, with the furnace-like heat or icy cold sandwiched between. Sure there are the bad times too. A feller gets awfully cold in a tent in the snow in the dead of winter and sweating his shirt off in the summer. But in the hottest part of summer have you ever seen a cowboy with a canteen? I've seen a lot of cowboys, but I never have. Why? Because they like to take the same beating that the horse is taking. They like to match themselves against nature, men like themselves, and horses. They like competition from any source. They take pride in physical strength and toughness. I like this life. I like to feel the splash of cold water against my face in the morning and the feel of the blankets of my unmade bed at night. I like the sleep that hits like a mallet when a chance to sleep comes after a hard day's work. The power that ripples through wiry, hard-earned muscle gives me a sort of pride. I just plain like the work.

Every day starts off pretty much the same. I figure that getting dressed is as good a way as any to start the day. First, the Levis go on over my long-Johns; then I put on two wool shirts and a jacket. After that come the boots and overshoes. Then I tie a big handkerchief around my neck and tuck it down into the collar of my jacket to keep in the heat. I buckle on my chaps, which take the place of two more pairs of longies, and I slip on one of those army caps with the ear flaps – a Stetson just doesn't do the job in the wintertime – and out I go. Here on the flats it's been at least fifteen below zero every morning since the first big snow. I grain the string of horses that I'm using, cake the milk cow, lame bull, crippled steers, calves, and whatever else is in the corral. If we're feeding hay I'll shake out about a bale for the whole works. All this winter there's been ice on the tank in the morning, so I break that and hustle to the house for eats.

Breakfast is always the same, but I haven't got tired of it yet. A couple of pancakes, some steak, eggs and coffee every morning no matter what time of year it is.

After breakfast I get back to the corrals and saddle up. I always use a hackamore in the wintertime, but Dee doesn't. A bit that's sticky cold can raise heck with a horse's mouth. If I'm using a bridle I always take it over to the water tank and get a good coating of ice on it before I put it into his mouth. I put the blankets on a horse differently in the winter than in the summer. In summer I put a hairpad on the bottom and the blanket on top. In the winter I do it the other way around.

I pack a .22 in the wintertime. It's not for wolves or anything like that, but for jackrabbits. The mink ranchers pay ten cents apiece for them during the winter. I shoot them while I'm checking and baling the cows and bulls. I make about thirty dollars a month just from rabbits that I shoot. That's about all the shooting I do, except that once in a while, when the meat supplies are running low, I'll pick off a little government beef.

The ranges are pretty well fenced, and there isn't much cow-driving in the wintertime. We just leave all of the gates open from one pasture to another and let them go where they want to. We weaned the calves about the middle of September, and now we've got all the calves in one big pasture. We count them every other day and cake them every day all winter long. The feed averages out about a small handful per each per day. The cows are scattered over 75,000 acres, about one fourth of which is flat and foothill country and the rest mountains. These cows have to be caked every now and then, too, although we don't keep too close a count on them. It's slow hard work for the horse. To cover twenty-five miles a day isn't bad that time of year in that country.

The mountains impress a feller after he gets to know them. When I've got a good level-headed horse under me, I like to stand on the top of a mountain during a thunderstorm and watch the lightning all around me. All that power and fury sure makes me feel small. I almost feel that I can shake hands with God in a position like that. It's a fool thing to do, and if you've ever seen a dead horse on a butte with his hooves curled up, you know why. I have not got hit yet though, and somehow I always feel better afterwards. If you've got a horse that will stick with you and stay quiet then, you know you've got a good one.

Every month or so, I get a chance to go into town with the other boys. Once in a great while we'll get drunk or get into a fight, but usually we just go to a show or something. I'm pretty much the peaceable type.

If we've saved up enough money, sometimes we'll go to one of the big winter rodeos. Fred came into the big money in bareback bronc riding last year. I like rodeos. I like to watch the good broncs, the different ways fellers do things, the rig's they use; and I have fun watching friends of mine putting up good rides or seeing some newcomer rope a steer and bust him in record time. Before Fred took the job as foreman of the ranch, he rodeoed around and made over eleven thousand in '52 and '53. He's shown me a lot about the business, but I'm still a long way from being as good as he is. The trip to town is fun and so are the rodeos, but I'm always happy to get back to the ranch. There a man can think without people butting in and holler when he feels like hollering; and there it's me with Mother Nature as my best gal and no enemies except the critters that I make that way.

"The basic property with which man is endowed of choosing for himself will always cause disagreement and therefore change."

Peter Smith

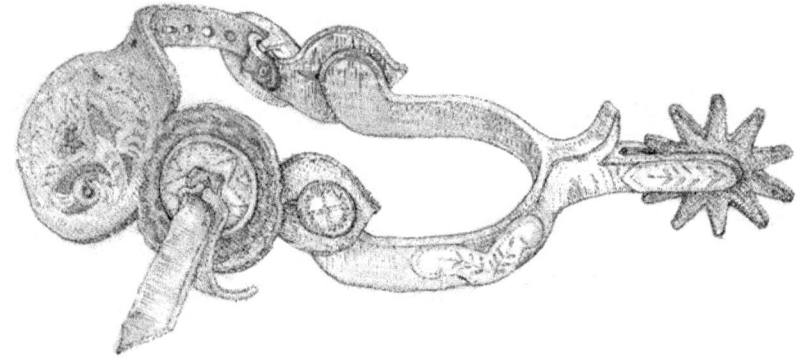

All My Love

$\mathcal{I}$ met her at a Cotillion dance. She wasn't the most beautiful or the cutest girl I know, but she had a personality the likeness of which I had never seen. She was natural in everything she did. There was no show of unfelt emotion or feeling, and she didn't force herself on you. There was a depth and indescribable deepness to her which my poor vocabulary lacks words to portray. She said what she felt but no more, and instilled in me an immediate liking for her.

Jane, a freckle-faced girl that I'd known in the sixth grade, was the only person outside of the family that I'd ever felt that way about before. I had given her my ring, she gave me her bracelet, and we went steady. I told her in my simple words that I loved her and wanted to marry her someday. She told me that I'd probably change my mind by the time I was that old and we'd look back at our puppy-love someday and laugh together about it. That made me stop and think, but it also made me angry with her, and, though I was surely sorry afterwards, I broke up our friendship. I never did get my little silver ring back nor she her bracelet. I am sure now that she had a lot more on the ball than I did.

Judy and I have a lot in common. She wants to live on a place in the country and raise horses and a family someday just as I do. I'm sure she's a good cook, although, I have never tasted any of her makings, and she's got everything that a man wants in a wife. Judy and I hit it off great from the first. We made a date for the fifth for a real nice dance. That was the best dance I've been to (almost) since I remember. The music and the same old crowd weren't any different, but she was with me, and that's all it took.

We left early and went to a little out-of-the-way place and had a glass of beer and a piece of apple pie. She looked old enough that she didn't need identification, and I was eighteen by a month anyway. We sat at a table in the corner and talked about everything and anything, people especially. She liked people in general a lot more than I do. I felt wonderfully warm inside in a way that I haven't felt since. I was sure that this was the real thing. We left the place and got into the car. I kissed her once lightly, and we started for home. She was snuggled close to me all the way to her house, but I didn't put my arm around her, because she wanted me to keep my eyes on the road.

When we stopped in front of her house, we talked some more. She was easy to talk to. I kissed her. There is nothing to compare to her kiss with, so warm and full of feeling was it. I walked her to the house, and after seeing her safely inside, I went back to the car.

She went to a church on the east side, and so I started going too. I was never much for going to church; but as I knelt beside her and prayed, I found myself closer to that certain something called God than I have ever been before.

The following days, weeks, and months seemed to go by so fast that I could not count them with the two of us taking every opportunity to be together. She had not found in me the substance that I knew in her, however, and we drifted apart. Now memories keep me warm, and I haven't been to a dance for months. My plans for the future are not changed, my work goes on with the same dogmatic regularity, and everything seems to be pretty much as usual; but there is something missing somewhere, and I've been doing too much thinking lately.

Cat Hunt

We Joness live back up in the big timber country north of Freeport. The woods are loaded with bobcats. They's a big creek running past our house. I decides that I'll just foller that creek way back into the woods. The creek is pretty big, and every once in a while it widens out at an elbow to make a nice pond for ducks and muskrat. Off to the sides is heavy timber and cut over places with second growth bushes where partridge hang out. I've got a .410 that's just about right for cat hunting – provided the cat ain't too big. Best of all, I got me a hound dog name of Betsy that figures she's pretty hot on anything from pink elephants to green mice – even though nobody else does. I call her one-shot Bess. (I don't know what she calls me.) I have to pick my shots pretty careful when she's with me, 'cause it seems I'm always hunting alone after the gun goes off first time.

Today I have my mind set on one thing, and that's cats. I start off tramping softly through the dry snow telling that old mutt of mine every now and then to leave those squirrels the *'()# alone. I come out on a place where the creek widens into a bog and spots me a cow moose. She was the mangiest cow moose I ever see in all my fourteen years of heavy squirrel hunting. She hadn't caught my smell, but I sure got a good one of her. I just stands there, and finally she gets a bead on me and looks at me like she had just swallered a cake of granma's lye soap, and I was to blame. I ain't scared though; I've got a good stout load of number four shot leveled right smack at the middle of her punkin haid, and I'm just handy to an easy-climbing tree.

Well, that old gal thinks it over and figures out that I plumb got the upper hand for now. She smashes off into the timber with the great loping strides of a wore-out bull in a bog hole.

Knowing that even a ferocious critter like that wouldn't dare take on a feller the likes of me, I take right out after her with brave little Bess slinkin' along behind me. These old cows know the country a lot better than a man. She'd probably take me into some better cat country than what I was going to find by myself.

Gerty, that's what I name my friend, took off on a trail through some second growth pines. A feller that's an old hand at tracking down everything from moose to meece the way I am, can manage to make out elephant tracks in fresh snow without too much trouble, provided that they aren't over an hour old. I follers them tracks for quite a while, until I comes to where it looks as though somebody has been follering a flat-footed deer or somethin'.

I decides to follow those tracks instead of the ones I have been. It might turn out to be somebody I know. I foller those tracks until the queerest thing happens! I find a place where they's two sets of man tracks. I knew that I really had something. I kept follering those tracks for almost an hour and was hot on the trail of a whole gang of fellers before long. I figgered that I better quit tracking them, or I would be sure to get into trouble, if one of them should happen to circle back and catch me snoopin'.

Old Bess seemed happy to get off to a fresh trail. It almost seemed as though she were bored with the whole thing. We hadn't been walking for long, before old Bess hit a trail of something that like to burned her nose off. She took off after whatever it was a-yowling and a-squawking and howlin' to beat all git out. Now old Bess may be a little wacky in the haid, but she don't whingding around like that unless she's really excititated. I took off at a whopa doodle run that covered the ground in a jiffy. I was plumb excititated too. Bess was about a half-mile away, hooting her haid off while she ran, and I was really goin' full tilt too; then the racket makers doubled back. I was near the creek, and when I crashed through the brush along-side of it, I saw a ruckus a little ways off up the creek on the other side. Old Bess had finally persuaded whatever it was that it was time to be taking to the air.

I saw the yaller tabby go a-streakin' up this big old pine. Afore he even stopped, I had cranked three loads of shot into his hide. He must have got mighty inspired by that, because he kep' a-runnin' clear on up and over the top. He did a whodingy of a dowhopper of a double somersaulting flip flop over into the bushes at the bottom. I thought he was probably plumb daid by then, but old Bess didn't. She hadn't run away this time, and when that cat landed there, she gummed him end to end. I hustled over thar afore she had tore the trophy hide plumb to pieces to examine the lion. I found that I had done something pretty unusual. I had shot me a bobcat with a long tail. The hide sure looked a lot more impressive off'n him than it did on.

I thought that Pa would be plumb tickled to see a cat like that. When Pa saw me with it, I thought he was goin' to lay me out. Seems Mrs. Beckman had been over to ask if har big yaller tiger cat had been over visiting. She said it was the first time that he had ever run away for so long. I was told that if I didn't bury the thing in six feet of quicksand that I was liable to get it whar it hurt the most. I just got through burying it, and I've been trying to figure out what that old gal was doing, raising bobcats and tigers.

"Bucking is hard on a horse though; it jars his every bone, raises havoc with his joints, and pulls his muscles besides taking a lot of energy. A good minute of that is approximately equal to a good day's work."

Peter Smith

What is Man?

Man is a competitive being in love, war, athletics, business, and almost everything. Each man has his own personal set of ethics which changes constantly with the arising of a new situation with which the old set of standards is incapable of coping. This being the case, new problems will arise constantly and stagnancy of the mind is most unlikely.

The human personality is a wonderful thing. No two people are exactly alike. One person will view a matter in one light and another in some other shade. When the matter is a large one, conflict is likely on a large scale which in turn brings about stimulation of new ideas. Even the smaller disagreements encourage competition. The basic property with which man is endowed of choosing for himself will always cause disagreement and strife, and therefore change.

The more hell and high water that people encounter, the more they seem to be a god; Billy Graham in England making the hit that he is. As there will always be unsolved problems, and questions and things to be accounted for, speculation of life after death, a boundless, perfect, supernatural God will always be needed and used.

Coyote Pete

Behind the chutes the boys was crouched
Their whole attention spent
On drawin' straws and hopin' for
A hoss as was hell-bent.

Jick drawed a hoss named Coyote Pete
Like in the comic strip
And stretched his legs and waited for
His turn to make the trip.

The doggin' came, the barebacks went
(The ropin' was plumb through.)
And then at last came saddle broncs and
One last swig 'o 'dew.

The saddle – she was cinched up tight
The flank strap was drawed down
Jick eased onto that bronc's back
And gave a look aroun'!

He tucked his hat and stuck his spurs
Into "Coyote's" shoulder blades
Then he whispered "Let 'im out,"
And things began to blaze.

That hoss went ten feet in the air
An' crashed into the fences
He whirled and bucked and kicked and ran
Like 's if he'd lost 'is senses!

But ol' Jick hung to like a burr
An' never give an inch
For since the very first he had
Been hangin' to the fence.

"No hour of life is wasted that is spent in the saddle."

Winston Churchill

About the Author

Abbott Pliny "Pete" Smith III was born June 16, 1938 in Augusta, Maine, USA. He was the second of five children born to Abbott Pliny Smith, II and Elizabeth Cooper Saunders Smith. In 1952, when Pete was 14 years old, his family moved to Denver, Colorado. Pete attended South High School in Denver. A teen who loved horses, Pete found his way to the local rodeo and ranches where he was befriended by seasoned cowboys and weathered wranglers. When Pete's parents returned to the east, Pete stayed behind, working as a ranch hand. He graduated high school in 1956. Following his love for animals, he attended Colorado State University and graduated with a degree in Veterinary Medicine in 1962. In 1963, Dr. Smith and his family, dogs, cat, and horses, moved to Athens, Ohio where he continued his veterinary career serving the Ohio Valley. As a skilled surgeon, revered for his work with horses, Dr. Smith opened Milliron Clinic. February 22, 2010, Pete died of complications due to a logging accident. Family and friends will forever remember Pete's love for life, his passion for horses, rolling laugh, hearty handshake, and skill as a world-class veterinarian.

On the Back Cover:

Top left: 1956. Peter Smith's South High School, Denver, Colorado, graduation picture.

Bottom right: Dr. Pete Smith astride his gelding, Unique, in the highlands of Middle Mountain, West Virginia. Picture courtesy of Rhonda and Eric Curfman, Pete's long-time riding companions. Eric writes, "This picture was taken in 2009 on private property owned since the late 1800's by the Arborgast family. It is on the county line of Randolph and Pocahontas, looking at the head of Gandy Creek, upstream of the Sinks of Gandy. Pete and I rode on this property for the first time in 1997. When seeing it for the first time, he commented on how it reminded him of Colorado. Anytime we traveled to this area to ride, he insisted on riding to this trail at least one day. Rhonda and I think of him every time we ride up there. Pete called it God's Country."

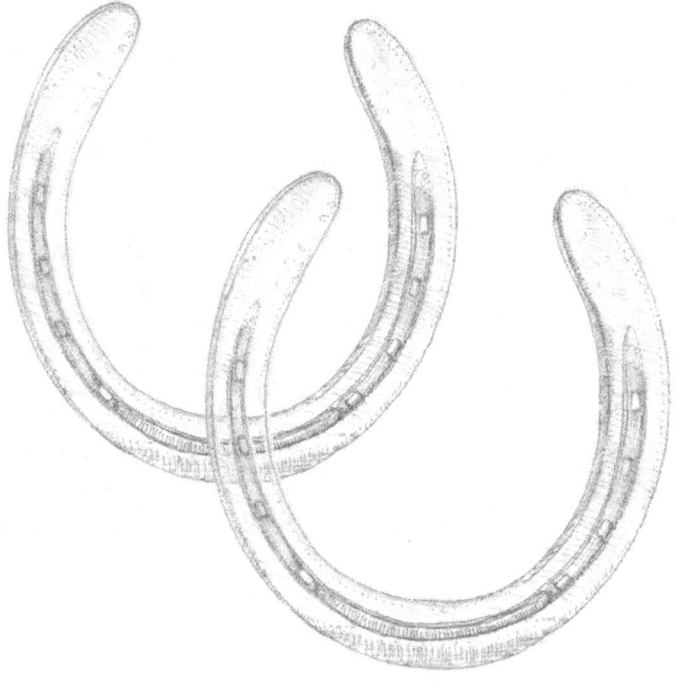